+
920
DAV

Davis

Women who changed history.
145861

WOMEN
WHO CHANGED HISTORY

WOMEN
WHO CHANGED HISTORY
FIVE FAMOUS QUEENS OF EUROPE

Mary L. Davis

LERNER PUBLICATIONS COMPANY
MINNEAPOLIS, MINNESOTA

To my daughter, Laura Eileen

LIBRARY OF CONGRESS CATALOGING IN PUBLICATION DATA

Davis, Mary Lee.
    Women who changed history: five famous queens of Europe.

(A Real World Book)
    CONTENTS: Eleanor of Aquitaine; Isabella of Spain;
Elizabeth I; Marie Antoinette; Catherine the Great.

1. Queens—Biography—Juvenile literature. I. Title.

D107.D38   940'.0992 [B]   74-11899
ISBN 0-8225-0638-6

Published simultaneously in Canada by J. M.
Dent & Sons (Canada) Ltd., Don Mills, Ontario

Manufactured in the United States of America

International Standard Book Number: 0-8225-0638-6
Library of Congress Catalog Card Number: 74-11899

Contents

These sculptured figures of Louis VII and Eleanor of Aquitaine stand at the western doorway of Chartres Cathedral in France.

Eleanor of Aquitaine (1122-1204)
Queen of France, Queen of England

Eleanor of Aquitaine, queen of France and queen of England, was the power behind many thrones. She influenced the reigns of four kings — two of them her husbands, and two of them her sons. The beautiful duchess of Aquitaine never found lasting happiness, but she became one of the first truly political women in history.

Born in 1122 in the prosperous duchy of Aquitaine, in what is now southern France, Eleanor was the daughter of Duke William. At the time of her birth, France was divided into many duchies, or independent states. Each was ruled by a duke, and each had a loose allegiance to the king of France. One of the largest and most powerful duchies of all, Aquitaine was in some ways more important than France itself.

Even as a child, Eleanor of Aquitaine was more interested in political and military problems than in what was considered "women's work." Slender and graceful, she excelled at horsemanship and archery. Duke William may have regretted not having a son, but as Eleanor grew up, he praised his good fortune in having a daughter like her. After her mother died, Eleanor developed an even closer relationship with her father. She went with him on frequent good-will tours through Aquitaine, carefully observing the skillful way he dealt with the people. Eleanor was very popular among the people of Aquitaine, and when Duke William died in 1137, they readily accepted her as their duchess.

There was one serious problem at the time of the duke's death. Eleanor was in love with a handsome young knight named Richard, but his status was considered too lowly for him to be the husband of a duchess. Duke William had worried about Eleanor's attachment to Richard, but he had done nothing to end it. After the duke died, however, some powerful members of his council decided that Eleanor could not be wasted on a mere knight. Beautiful, rich, and politically important, she was a prize that should be saved for the highest bidder.

Eleanor's love for Richard was doomed. There is a story that he was murdered right in front of Eleanor's horrified eyes one night when the lovers tried to meet each other secretly. At any rate, Richard vanished. A short time later, 15-year-old Eleanor of Aquitaine was married to Prince Louis of France, the heir to the French throne. Politically, at least, the marriage was a brilliant move. By uniting the large duchy of Aquitaine with the domain of the French crown, it offset the holdings of the duke of Normandy, Geoffrey Plantagenet. (Normandy, like Aquitaine, was one of the most powerful duchies in western Europe, and the war-loving Plantagenet was always seeking more lands.)

Days after Eleanor married him, 18-year-old Prince Louis became Louis VII, king of France. (His father, Louis VI, had died after ruling France for almost 30

A woodcut of Louis VII, the crusader-king who ruled France from 1137 to 1180

years.) Louis was a shy, quiet, extremely religious young man. He was intelligent, but he was dominated almost completely by two influential clergymen named Odo and Bernard.

Eleanor, now a queen, found the French court at Paris dull and somber. Her closest companion there was her waiting woman, Amaria. There were many times when Queen Eleanor, with her knowledge of Aquitaine politics, might have helped Louis rule his newly acquired holding. But the king's advisers would not allow Eleanor to participate in political matters because they felt she was a bad influence on her husband. In their eyes, the queen was a pleasure-seeking woman of questionable morals.

Louis VII was probably as much in love with his beautiful wife as a man of his nature could be. But he was cold, unromantic, and unworldly. Eleanor, a passionate woman in the bloom of youth, felt cheated in her marriage. "I thought I had married a king," she once said, "but I find I have married a monk!" Receiving little attention from her husband, Eleanor spent many hours daydreaming with her maid, Amaria, about courtly love and knights in shining armor. The queen often ridiculed the French court for being stiff and formal, and she wasted little time in filling it with music, laughter, and the romantic songs of adoring poets. King Louis did not approve of his wife's behavior, but he put up with it, just the same.

Queen Eleanor was a bright, well-educated woman, and she was drawn almost at once to the schools of Paris. Here, small groups of scholars from all over Europe studied theology, philosophy, and civil law with their masters. Women were allowed to listen to the lectures and debates, but they were forbidden to participate in them. This frustrated the outspoken Eleanor, and whenever she attended the schools, she had to bite her tongue to keep from talking.

Finally, something happened to relieve the queen's boredom. For many years, the Christians of western Europe had been trying to recapture the Holy Land from the Turks, the war-loving Moslems who had captured Jerusalem in 1071. Now, in 1147, Louis VII was persuaded by his countrymen and religious advisers to organize the second military expedition, or crusade, into Palestine. Eleanor had no burning desire to join the Holy War, but she didn't want to stay at home while her husband made the pilgrimage to Palestine.

Determined to have her own way, Queen Eleanor begged the king to let her and a group of her ladies accompany the men on the crusade. The king's advisers were strongly opposed, but Eleanor had a trump card in her hand. The men of Aquitaine had not been enthusiastic recruits, and Eleanor insisted that they would join the crusade more readily if she set an example for them by joining the expedition herself. At first, clergymen like Odo and Bernard were outraged at the thought of having the queen along on the crusade. But they couldn't ignore her argument, and they finally agreed to let her go.

Delighted, Eleanor began making preparations for the journey to Palestine. To the dismay of the men who tried to convince them that the crusade was not going to be a pleasure trip, Eleanor and her ladies packed trunks full of pretty clothes and dressed up in the armor of Amazons, or female warriors. Then, after all the preparations were made, Louis and Eleanor set sail for the East.

Once on the way, across the sea and over mountains and deserts, Eleanor and her band of Amazons found out how right the men had been. But they wouldn't admit it. Camped in cold and dirty tents at night, they brushed their tangled hair and smeared lotions on their wind-burned faces. They had little opportunity to wear their lovely clothes, and they eventually had to throw away most of their trunks.

Eleanor and Louis were deliberately separated during most of the long journey (the king's "keepers" saw to that), and they worried about each other constantly. They were finally reunited when they reached Antioch, a Christian stronghold on the eastern shore of the Mediterranean Sea. Welcoming them to the city was Eleanor's good-looking uncle, Raymond of Toulouse, prince of Antioch. Prince Raymond wined and dined Eleanor and her ladies, and he ordered new wardrobes for all of them.

Queen Eleanor enjoyed the merrymaking at Antioch, and she flirted openly with her handsome uncle. Naturally, the queen's conduct outraged King Louis and his religious counselors Odo and Bernard. When Louis finally insisted on leaving Antioch, Prince Raymond advised him not to attack Jerusalem. "Be content with putting the Turks down in Antioch," Raymond told him. But Louis would not listen. He was determined to leave.

The crusaders are shown entering the Holy City of Jerusalem in this engraving from a 12th-century manuscript.

Siding with her uncle's position, Eleanor refused to accompany her husband to Jerusalem. In response, King Louis said he would force her to go. As long as she had come this far, he declared, she would be with him when he entered the Holy City. Eleanor threatened to divorce the king if he made her go, but it made no difference. Desperate to win in this showdown, King Louis had the queen carried into Jerusalem against her will.

Angry and insulted, Queen Eleanor began to despise her husband. When the attack on Jerusalem went badly and had to be abandoned, she did not console the king. She was ready to go home, and with good reason—she was pregnant for the second time.

Once back in Paris, the queen began to ponder the miserable state of her marriage. So far, she had failed to give the king a male heir. Her first child had been a daughter, Marie. If her second child was a boy, she would try harder to make the marriage work, Eleanor decided. But the baby was another girl, named Alix.

After the birth of Alix, Eleanor and Louis grew further and further apart. Bored with the French court and disgusted with her pious husband, Eleanor again began thinking about a divorce. This pleased the king's advisers, for they had never considered Eleanor a suitable wife for the king. "She is too worldly and bold," they said, "and she is not even capable of producing a son!" Finally, in 1152, Louis and Eleanor were divorced on the grounds that they were fourth cousins. Nothing could have pleased Eleanor more.

Eleanor wanted to take her two little girls back with her to Aquitaine, but she was not allowed to. With tears in her eyes, she kissed Marie and Alix goodbye and gave them some trinkets to remember her by. "I can't come back here," she told them, "but you can come to visit me in Aquitaine."

Her title of queen stripped away with the divorce, Eleanor returned home to Aquitaine after 15 years in the dreary French court. The wealthy duchess entertained her old friends in a grand manner, and her luxurious court at Poitiers Palace soon became known as a "court of love." By teaching knights to treat their ladies with gentlemanly honor and devotion, the duchess of Aquitaine helped elevate the position of women. At the same time, she promoted the arts by welcoming poets, musicians, and artists to her palace. The high quality of court life and courtly manners cultivated by Eleanor at Poitiers Palace did not go unnoticed. Eventually, in fact, Eleanor's illustrious court became the norm by which all the leading courts of Europe were judged.

More attractive than ever, the green-eyed divorcee had many admirers, all of them seeking her hand in marriage. One of her most handsome suitors was Henry Plantagenet, the 18-year-old son of Geoffrey, the duke of Normandy. Young Henry had long admired Eleanor, and after his father died, he asked the duchess to become his bride. He could offer her nothing at the moment, he explained, but all that would soon change. He would become king of England after his uncle, King Stephen, died. And if Eleanor married him, she would be England's next queen.

Eleanor found the tall, red-haired young duke of Normandy very appealing, and she fell in love with him almost at once. Gay, worldly, and passionate, he was the complete opposite of Eleanor's first husband, Louis VII. But he was so very young; Eleanor was 11 years his

Eleanor of Aquitaine encouraged knights to treat women with honor, generosity, and devotion. The knight in this illustration pays homage to his lady before competing in a tournament.

senior—almost old enough to be his mother! Despite her misgivings, Henry was very persistent. He wanted Eleanor's hand in marriage, and he finally got it. In May of 1152—less than a year after her divorce from King Louis—Eleanor of Aquitaine married Henry Plantagenet, the future Henry II of England.

In contrast to her life with King Louis, Eleanor's life with Henry Plantagenet was fast-paced and exciting. The energetic duke was always on the move, and Eleanor went

An engraving of Henry
II, based on his tomb
effigy

with him on frequent trips throughout Normandy and
Aquitaine. Then, less than six months after they were
married, Eleanor gave birth to her first son by Henry. The
child was named William, after Eleanor's father.

With the death of King Stephen in November 1154,
Henry and Eleanor set sail for England. They were
crowned as the new king and queen of England on Decem-
ber 19, 1154. Once established in Windsor Palace, King
Henry got to work straightening out what he called
"Stephen's legacy of muck and muddle." At the same
time, Queen Eleanor concentrated on improving the
quality of the English court, which she found crude and
unpolished. She also gave Henry a lot of free advice on
ruling his kingdom. Unlike Louis VII, King Henry often
accepted Eleanor's helping hand.

Eleanor of Aquitaine,
in an engraving based
on her tomb effigy

Between 1154 and 1167, Eleanor gave birth to seven more children. After William, who died in infancy, came young Henry. Then came Richard (the namesake of Eleanor's long-dead lover), Geoffrey, young Eleanor, Joanna, and finally John. All of them were outgoing children, but Richard led the pack. Eleanor praised his aggressive traits, and she boasted that he was a "natural leader." It was unfair, she sometimes thought, that he was not the heir to the throne instead of his older brother, Henry, who had a much weaker personality.

The next years were very busy ones for both the king and the queen of England. Henry spent much of his time reshaping England's laws and institutions. A capable administrator and judicial reformer, he earned the name of Henry the Lawgiver. He was also busy traveling throughout his duchies and putting down frequent uprisings on the Welsh border. More and more, Henry and Eleanor were going their separate ways. Busy with her children and court life, Eleanor spent much less time with her husband than she had during the early days of their marriage.

When the three eldest sons of Eleanor and Henry were in their teens, the king gave them their titles and let them try their hand at ruling his duchies in France. Young Henry got Normandy; Geoffrey was given Britanny; and Richard, at Eleanor's insistence, got her treasured homeland of Aquitaine—clearly the best prize of all.

The year was 1170. Eleanor had just returned from a visit to Aquitaine, beaming with pride at the way her favorite son was handling things, when she first noticed the change in her husband. He seemed distant, quiet, preoccupied. At first, Eleanor thought that the king's strange mood had something to do with the Becket affair.

Thomas à Becket had been Henry's friend, chancellor, and later, archbishop. Henry's attempt to gain control of the church in England led to a bitter quarrel between the king and Becket, a man Eleanor never liked because of his extreme piety. After hearing Henry rave against Becket, four of the king's knights murdered the archbishop while he was at prayer in the cathedral of Canterbury. Henry claimed that he had not actually wanted Becket killed, and he took all the blame for the archbishop's death.

But it wasn't the Becket affair that accounted for the change in Henry. It was another affair—his love affair with Rosamond Clifford. A beautiful woman many years younger than Queen Eleanor, Rosamond Clifford was the king's mistress for many years without the queen's

The murder of Thomas à Becket, taken from a manuscript in the British Museum

knowledge. When Eleanor finally learned the facts, she went to Rosamond's cottage intending to have it out with her. Legend has it that when she got there, the queen was so envious of Rosamond's youth and beauty that she poisoned her.

There is no proof that Eleanor killed her rival. But it is known that after she learned of Henry's unfaithfulness, she grew to despise him. For many years, the king and queen of England did not even live together. And at one point, Henry had Eleanor locked up in a castle so she would not be able to interfere in his life.

Eleanor never forgave the king for his infidelity. Spiteful and hurt, she encouraged her sons (especially Richard) to revolt against their father. In an attempt to take over Henry's lands, Richard, Geoffrey, and young Henry allied themselves with Eleanor's ex-husband, King Louis of France. Henry II spent the rest of his life fighting them, and when he died in 1189, he died a heartbroken and embittered man. (Even his favorite son, John, had turned against him for personal gain.)

Since young Henry preceded Henry II in death, the throne went to Richard. This must have made Eleanor very happy; at last, she saw her favorite son take his place as the king of England. Unfortunately, Eleanor saw very little of Richard during his 10-year reign, for he spent most of that time in the Holy Land, fighting in the Third Crusade. In Richard's absence, his brother John ruled England.

If Richard I was an irresponsible king, he was also a courageous warrior. As a result of his many daring victories against the Turks, he earned the name of Richard the Lion-Hearted. Then, after the Third Crusade ended,

A heroic statue of Richard the Lion-Hearted, London

he was taken prisoner by the emperor of Austria, who demanded a huge ransom for his release. Eleanor promptly paid the ransom, and her son was set free. Five years later, in 1199, Richard the Lion-Hearted was killed during a minor battle in Normandy. When Eleanor learned of his death, she went into a long period of mourning. Richard had been the one great love of her life, and now he was gone, taken away from her by some faceless enemy.

John, who had been reigning all along, was officially crowned as king of England after Richard's death. King John was a cruel and foolish ruler, and he made many enemies among the nobles and religious leaders of England during his reign. Eventually, he was forced to sign the Magna Carta, the charter in which English nobles demanded their rights.

An engraving of King John, who reigned from 1199 to 1216

Eleanor had never liked John; he was not nearly so handsome as Richard, and he had always been weak and deceitful. Nor did John like his mother; her partiality for Richard had always been obvious to him. Left alone with John, the aging Queen Eleanor found little happiness in her last years. She attempted to help John rule England, but the king would not allow her to meddle in his affairs. As Eleanor grew older, she turned away from John and became more involved with her daughters and grand-children, many of whom married into prominent European ruling families.

In spite of losing the love of those dearest to her — either through death or through disenchantment — Eleanor of Aquitaine never lost her zest for living. Troubadours were still singing of her beauty when she was well beyond 60, and she remained a powerful influence in European politics right up until the time of her death. Glamorous, stately, aggressive, self-assured — Eleanor was always every inch a queen.

The tomb effigies of Eleanor and Richard I. Not shown here is Henry II, who lies to Eleanor's right.

Eleanor of Aquitaine, wife and mother of kings, died in the year 1204. She was 82 at the time—a tremendous age in those days. Buried in Normandy, she lies forever between those whom she also set apart in life: her unfaithful husband, Henry, and her favorite son, Richard.

A portrait of Isabella, the Catholic queen, by B. Bermejo

Isabella of Spain (1451-1504)
The Catholic Queen

Isabella of Spain, whose name is linked forever with the names of a powerful king and a poverty-stricken sailor, was a woman of sharp contrasts. She was proud of her role as a wife and mother, but she preferred fighting wars to staying at home. She sought wealth and luxury, yet she forced herself and her family to endure many hardships. Known as the Catholic queen, Isabella was one of the most religious women of the 15th century—and one of the most bigoted. Her life was characterized by triumph and tragedy; her reign, by greatness and disgrace.

Born in 1451, Isabella was the daughter of King John II, ruler of the Spanish kingdom of Castile. Spain was not a united nation in those days. Instead, it was made up of several independent kingdoms, the most important ones being Castile, Aragon, and Granada. While both Castile and Aragon were Christian kingdoms, the southern kingdom of Granada belonged to the Moors—Moslems from northern Africa who had invaded Spain in the eighth century. Isabella was raised to hate the non-Christian Moors, and her lifelong ambition was to drive them out and make Spain an entirely Christian nation.

Isabella's father, King John, was an easygoing, pleasure-loving man. But her mother was a high-strung woman who often suffered spells of hysteria. Early in life, Isabella learned how to control her feelings and to fend for herself. A very well-behaved child, she was almost "too good to be natural," according to her nursemaid.

When King John died in 1455, Isabella's half brother, Henry, became the king of Castile. Henry was a greedy, self-seeking man, and Isabella's mother did not trust him (she and her stepson had never gotten along). As a result, she took her four-year-old daughter, Isabella, and her young son, Alfonso, away from Henry's court soon after Henry was crowned king.

For the most part, Isabella's childhood was dull and uneventful. Since her mother had taken her to the little town of Arevalo, far from King Henry's court, Isabella grew up without knowing the luxuries of a Spanish princess. A great deal of attention was devoted to her religious training, and the young Isabella soon became a devout Roman Catholic. One day, she decided, she would help rid her country of the Moors and make Spain a wholly Catholic nation. This was to be Isabella's greatest mission in life. Unbendable in her beliefs, she had a natural instinct to be a crusader.

When Isabella was still a young girl, something wonderful happened to her: she became engaged to marry Prince Ferdinand, the handsome young heir to the kingdom of Aragon. Isabella was given such a glowing description of her future husband that she fell deeply in love with him.

Even before seeing him, she was sure that Ferdinand was the only man in the world for her. This conviction remained with Isabella always, even when her marriage to Ferdinand had its problems.

Isabella knew that as Ferdinand's wife, she would become the queen of Aragon one day. But she never dreamed that she would become queen of her own country, Castile. After all, she reasoned, when King Henry died, the throne would automatically go to her younger brother, Alfonso. Still, Isabella's mother insisted that she be prepared for the possibility of becoming the queen of Castile. Perhaps that is why Isabella was such a dignified and well-behaved child.

In 1467, Alfonso died, making Princess Isabella the next in line for the crown of Castile. Two years later, in 1469, Isabella married Prince Ferdinand of Aragon.

This woodcut of a 15th-century marriage ceremony was made about 30 years after the marriage of Ferdinand and Isabella, who exchanged vows in 1469.

Isabella had idolized the prince for more than 10 years. Now, upon seeing him for the first time, she gasped with delight. It was as if he had stepped out of her dreams. A year younger than Isabella, Ferdinand was tall, fair, and filled with youthful self-confidence. Isabella had loved him for so long; now, she hoped that he would love her as well. If he did, Isabella told herself, she would have everything that a young woman could possibly want.

The first few years of Isabella's life with Ferdinand were very exciting ones. In 1470 Isabella gave birth to her first child, a daughter. Four years later King Henry died, making 23-year-old Isabella the queen of Castile. Then, in 1479, Ferdinand's father died, making Ferdinand the new king of Aragon. The two Christian kingdoms of Castile and Aragon were thus united against the Moorish kingdom of Granada. Now Isabella had a splendid vision of herself and Ferdinand—united in love and ideals— launching a victorious campaign to defeat the Moors and to unite Spain. This, Isabella believed, was God's plan for her and Ferdinand.

As the co-rulers of Castile and Aragon, Isabella and Ferdinand were equals. King Ferdinand loved his strong-willed wife and supported most of her goals, but he resented her great power. "I will teach her who is master," he boasted to his advisers, "and see to it that she casts away her pride and primness." But Queen Isabella was not a servant girl—and certainly not a woman to be taken lightly. Despite her passionate love for Ferdinand, she never forgot that she was his equal. When the problems of ruling together created bitter disagreements, Isabella became dismayed. "If I win the argument and lose your love," she once told Ferdinand, "I have lost

Isabella as a young queen

anyway." Still, it was never easy for the queen to give in to her husband on any point.

If the union of Isabella and Ferdinand was not always a happy one, it was at least a successful one, from a political standpoint. Together, the co-rulers of Castile and Aragon presented a strong force against the Moors. From 1480 onward, their campaign against the Moslem invaders of Spain gained more and more momentum. Both Ferdinand and his courageous wife loved the excitement of war. And, to Isabella at least, the war against the Moors was a holy crusade, with Christian against non-Christian, good against evil.

In appearance, Queen Isabella was very feminine and fragile. Biographers state that she was fine-featured and pretty, with auburn hair, perfect skin, and elegantly tiny hands and feet. Like most women, she loved fine clothes and beautiful jewelry. But Queen Isabella liked the look and feel of a suit of armor just as much, and she eagerly accompanied her husband on his military expeditions against the Moors. She stayed with him for months at a time, doing without luxuries and even basic necessities. The frail-looking "warrior queen" resented any suggestion that she was weak or inferior because she was a woman, and she scorned any special considerations.

During the long period when Isabella was waging war against the Moors, she managed to give birth to 10 children. Of these, only five survived infancy. Isabella was on the road with her troops when she had her last child, Catherine. Thirty-four years old, the queen was at an age when childbearing could be dangerous. But the birth was an easy one, and the baby was healthy. In a matter of days, Isabella took up her arms again, moving on to further victories against the Moors.

Hauled from one army camp to the other, the children of Isabella and Ferdinand scarcely knew a life without war. Tattered clothes were handed down from one child to the next, and there was little luxury or glamour in their young lives. Isabella might have left them at home, but she wanted her children beside her and Ferdinand—even if it meant taking them along on dangerous military expeditions. This way, she was able to supervise their education and upbringing. More than anything, Queen Isabella wanted to instill her religious and moral beliefs in her children. "Put all your faith and trust in God," she told them, "for everything that happens is His will." (The God-fearing queen also concerned herself with the morality of her soldiers, requiring them to attend religious services in the camps, and forbidding them to drink, swear, and gamble.)

Isabella and Ferdinand both placed a great deal of hope in their only son, Juan, born in 1478. They saw in his future the fulfillment of all their dreams and ambitions. One day, they believed, Juan would reign over a strong and united Spain; a Catholic Spain, free of the detested Moors.

Next to Juan, Isabella's favorite child was her daughter Juana (the queen had three other daughters: Isabella, Maria, and Catherine). Juana was a very lovely child—and a very troubled one, as well. Like Isabella's mother, she was temperamental, high-strung, and subject to frequent fits of hysteria and depression. Queen Isabella lavished her attention upon the girl—often at the expense of her other children—and for a time, Juana's condition seemed to improve. But after marrying Philip, archduke of Austria, and bearing him a son, Juana went insane. Following her husband's death in 1506, Juana "the Mad" was locked up in a remote country castle, where no one would see her. This drastic step was taken by her own father, King Ferdinand.

Fortunately, Queen Isabella did not live to see her favorite daughter put away. But before she died, the queen suffered the tragic loss of her only son. Never a healthy child, Juan died in 1497, at the age of 19. After his death, the grief-stricken Queen Isabella took to wearing the rough habit of a nun. She became so moody and shrewish that King Ferdinand could no longer tolerate her presence. Seeking the company of other women, the king became openly unfaithful.

Eventually, Queen Isabella came to realize that Ferdinand was not the heroic life-partner of her girlhood dreams. Cynical and embittered, she lectured Catherine, her youngest daughter, on the pitfalls of love and marriage. "Enter the convent," she urged her daughter. "Escape from all the misery and sorrow." But Catherine —better known as Catherine of Aragon—ignored her mother's advice and became the first wife of Henry VIII of England. (How right Isabella had been!)

What with her son's death, Juana's worsening illness, and the deterioration of her marriage, Isabella of Spain suffered greatly during her final years. But before her life turned into a Greek tragedy, the queen enjoyed at least two brilliant triumphs. The first occurred on January 2, 1492, when the Moors were finally forced to surrender Granada. Victorious, Ferdinand and Isabella hastily moved into magnificent Alhambra Palace, in the heart of Granada. There was great rejoicing throughout Spain, and many honors were bestowed upon Ferdinand and Isabella.

Queen Isabella had succeeded in defeating the Moors, but she wasn't satisfied. To Isabella, the Catholic queen, *any* religious beliefs other than her own were intolerable. So, not long after driving the Moors out of Spain, she signed an edict ordering *all* non-Christians to either leave Spain or become Christians. Thousands of Jews and Moslems (and even some bewildered Roman Catholics) were eventually questioned on their beliefs by the Spanish Inquisition, the religious tribunal established by Isabella back in 1480. Those who did not give the right answers were tortured or put to death. Unfortunately, the Spanish Inquisition lasted for hundreds of years, causing a relent-

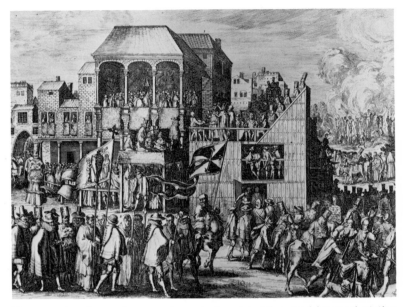

Thousands of people were branded as heretics and burned at the stake by the Spanish Inquisition, the religious tribunal established by Isabella in 1480.

less wave of religious repression. Of all Isabella's legacies to Spain, the Inquisition was by far the worst.

Another monumental event—a much more constructive one—also took place in 1492, while Queen Isabella was still residing in Alhambra Palace. It was then and there that the name of an ambitious young sailor became forever linked with Isabella's. The sailor was, of course, Christopher Columbus.

Born in Genoa, Italy, in 1451, Columbus was a man with a dream. Convinced that the world was round, not flat, he believed that he could find a shorter sea route to the East by sailing west. For many years, he tried to sell

Christopher Columbus

his plan to the leading monarchs of Europe in the hopes that they would finance his expedition. He appealed to John II of Portugal, Henry VII of England, and Charles VIII of France, but with no success. Though greedy for the gold and spices of the East, the rulers of Europe thought it impossible to reach the Indies by sailing west. "It can't be done," they said. "Only a madman would try such a thing!"

Columbus first approached Queen Isabella with his plan in 1485. If she would supply him with ships and supplies, he told her, he would make Spain the wealthiest nation in the world. Impressed with Columbus's idealism and self-confidence, Isabella listened to him politely. What appealed to her most was the possibility of great wealth for Spain, a country poor in natural resources. If Columbus succeeded, she mused, Spain would acquire the

Ferdinand of Spain

bountiful riches of the East. Isabella was intrigued. But since she was still fighting the Moors, she was in no position to do business with Columbus. "Come back when I have won the war," she told him. "Then I shall consider your venture more thoroughly."

Now, some seven years later, Columbus journeyed to Granada, where Ferdinand and Isabella were celebrating their hard-won victory over the Moors. In a do-or-die effort, Columbus again appealed to the queen to finance his expedition to the East. Isabella gave Columbus her undivided attention, but King Ferdinand was less enthusiastic. As Columbus talked excitedly about his plans, the king estimated the cost of the expedition. "Too much!" he declared. "Far too much!"

Isabella swiftly silenced her husband. "If the master of Aragon has no imagination," she said, "then I shall act on behalf of my own kingdom of Castile!" Ferdinand cringed at the attack, and Isabella became even more determined. Yet, she still had some doubts about financing Columbus's voyage. The war had nearly depleted the royal treasury, and now Columbus was asking for over $14,000 in ships and supplies. Could Spain afford to gamble with this much money? Isabella wasn't sure.

Columbus urged the queen on, but it was useless; Isabella was still plagued with doubt. Finally, Columbus challenged her. If the queen of Spain was not courageous enough to back him, he said, he was certain that the king of France would. Columbus was bluffing, of course, but Isabella had no way of knowing this. And she had *never* been one to back down from a challenge. So, putting aside her doubts, Queen Isabella at last agreed to finance Columbus's expedition.

Legend has it that Isabella pawned all her jewels to raise the money for the historic voyage. It is more likely, however, that she persuaded the royal treasurer to finance the venture. At any rate, Columbus set sail for the Indies on August 3, 1492, with a fleet of three ships and a total of 90 men. Two months later, on October 12, he discovered the island of San Salvador, in the Bahamas. Instead of reaching the Indies—as he believed he had—Christopher Columbus had discovered the New World!

Columbus returned home to Spain without the wealth he had promised, but with dazzling reports of the land he had discovered. If Queen Isabella was disappointed, she did not show it. She had shared in Columbus's bold adventure, and now she shared in his triumph. With Isabella's support, Columbus made three more voyages to the New World, discovering the islands of Puerto Rico and Jamaica, and the continents of North and South America. On the island of Hispaniola ("Little Spain"), Columbus established the first European colony in the New World. He named it "Isabela," after the queen who had helped him realize his lifelong dream.

As Spain's colonies in the New World grew, Spain became the most powerful nation in Europe. Isabella's place in history was secure. She had gambled on the dream of an ambitious young sailor, and she had won. Had Isabella not gambled, the course of history might have been vastly different.

After a courageous and eventful life, Isabella of Spain died in 1504, at the age of 53. She had devoted herself to her kingdom and to her church, and she had made Spain a great, united nation. Other rulers would follow her, but never again would Spain have so ardent a champion of its causes.

Elizabeth I, about 1592, by M. Gheeraerts the Younger

Elizabeth I (1533-1603)
A Greater Ruler, A Greater Nation

"Elizabeth will be a far greater ruler than you, and she will reign over a far greater nation!" shouted the slender, dark-haired young woman. Her husband slammed the door and stormed out in a rage. His face was as red as his beard.

The year was 1536. Henry VIII of England had just visited his second wife, Anne Boleyn, for the last time. A prisoner in the Tower of London, Anne was awaiting execution for alleged adultery and high treason. Henry had offered her a chance to live: he had asked her to divorce him and leave for France, to live in exile; he had asked her to take their three-year-old daughter, Elizabeth Tudor, with her, thereby renouncing all of Elizabeth's rights as heir to the kingdom. But Anne Boleyn had refused.

Big, blustery King "Hal" had once loved Anne desperately. In fact, his determination to divorce his first wife —Catherine of Aragon—and marry Anne Boleyn had resulted in an action that rocked England, and all of Europe. When Pope Clement VII refused to grant him a

Henry VIII

divorce from Catherine of Aragon, King Henry became enraged. Claiming that the pope had no authority over England, he broke away from the Roman Catholic church and established a separate religious body, the Church of England, with himself as its head. One of the first acts of the Church of England was to grant Henry VIII a divorce from Catherine of Aragon.

Free of his first wife, Henry married the beautiful Anne Boleyn early in 1533. A few months later, in September of 1533, Anne Boleyn gave birth to a daughter, Elizabeth Tudor. Although Elizabeth was destined to become England's greatest ruler, her birth was a bitter disappointment to King Henry, for he had long desired a son—a male heir to follow him as king of England. When, after three years of marriage, Anne Boleyn had still failed to give Henry a son, she fell from the king's favor. Obsessed

Anne Boleyn

with his desire for a male heir, and certain that his first two marriages had been cursed, Henry VIII now sought to cast Anne Boleyn aside and marry an even younger woman, Jane Seymour.

The people of England had never loved or accepted Henry's second wife. Most of them considered Anne Boleyn haughty, and some of them believed she was a sorceress. Aware of his people's sentiments, Henry VIII guessed that his popularity would be strengthened if he ended his marriage to Anne. But the marriage was binding. Henry had said so himself, speaking as the supreme head of the Church of England. Certainly, he could not contradict himself by having the marriage annulled! And it would be useless to ask Anne for a divorce; she would never agree to such a thing, for she liked being queen far too well.

Finally, Henry found a way to rid himself of his unwanted wife. Charges of adultery and treason were drummed up against Anne, and several of her alleged lovers were tortured into signing false confessions. When her trial was held, Anne Boleyn was found guilty and sentenced to die. The queen was astounded. She could not believe that Henry would allow her sentence to be carried out.

As the date for Anne Boleyn's execution drew near, Henry had second thoughts. Recalling how he had once loved Anne, he decided to find a face-saving way to spare her life. At last, he went to the Tower of London and told Anne that he would set her free if she would agree to divorce him and leave England, taking Elizabeth with her. But Anne Boleyn had never been a compromiser, and she scoffed at the king's offer. "I would rather die than give you a chance to deny Elizabeth her birthright!" she declared. "If I live as you suggest, it will be without honor. If I die, it will be for a good cause!"

As Henry stormed out of the room, cursing, Anne Boleyn fell to the floor and wept. "What will become of my little girl when I am gone?" she sobbed. "What will become of her?"

Anne Boleyn was beheaded on May 19, 1536. For a long time afterward, it seemed as if she had died in vain. Henry VIII married Jane Seymour one day after Anne's execution; a short time later, Anne Boleyn's daughter, three-year-old Elizabeth Tudor, was banished from the king's sight. All but disinherited, the saucy, red-haired little princess was sent away to an obscure rural castle, with only a governess to care for her.

In 1537, Jane Seymour gave Henry VIII a much-longed-for son, Edward. Overcome with fatherly joy and pride, Henry sent for his two other children: Mary Tudor, his daughter by Catherine of Aragon; and Elizabeth Tudor, his daughter by Anne Boleyn. When Edward was christened, four-year-old Elizabeth was allowed to march in the procession with her half sister, Mary. She was also given the honor of holding Edward's christening robe. This was the closest Princess Elizabeth had ever been to the pomp and pageantry of her father's court.

Soon after Edward's christening, Elizabeth was again dismissed from Henry's court. Mary Tudor, the king's eldest daughter, fared much better. Her mother had died by now, and Henry, beset with guilt, decided to let Mary remain with him. More than this, he passed an act that put her ahead of Elizabeth in the line of royal succession. This meant that of Henry's three children, Elizabeth would be the *last* to inherit the crown, running behind both Edward and Mary.

A castaway, young Elizabeth Tudor was raised by a governess in a country house some 150 miles away from Henry's court. If she received little affection from her father, she received even less from him in the way of material things. Letters from Elizabeth's governess pleaded for money, for clothes. "The poor child has nothing to wear," she wrote. "She has neither gown, nor kirtle, nor petticoat." But Henry, unconcerned with Elizabeth's needs, simply tossed the letters aside.

Elizabeth was denied many things as a girl, but she at least received a good education. A brilliant student, she mastered such diverse languages as Latin, Flemish, Greek, and French. She also studied history, mathematics, geography—and even architecture! Elizabeth's love of learning made her an avid reader; it also made her one of England's most knowledgeable and sharp-witted rulers.

In 1543, when Elizabeth was 10, King Henry took his sixth and last wife, Catherine Parr. At the queen's request, Elizabeth was allowed to return to the royal household. Princess Elizabeth couldn't have been more delighted. She was devoted to her half brother, Edward, and she took an immediate liking to Queen Catherine, who proved herself to be a kind and understanding stepmother. But above all, Elizabeth loved and adored her father, the king. She was often puzzled by his bad treatment of her, but she never wavered in her admiration for him. In many ways, they were much alike—shrewd, outspoken, vain, and forceful.

Unfortunately, Elizabeth got to spend only a brief time with her father. For on January 28, 1547, King Henry died, leaving the crown to his nine-year-old son, Edward. Six years later, King Edward died of consumption, leaving the crown to Mary Tudor. The year was 1553, and Elizabeth Tudor was now 20 years old. Already, she had suffered the loss of her mother, her father, and her closest companion, Edward.

Mary Tudor, Elizabeth's half sister, was 37 years old when she ascended the throne. A devout Catholic, Mary had long ago decided that she would avenge her mother, Catherine of Aragon, by restoring the Roman Catholic church in England. Now that she was queen, she became obsessed with this goal. She abolished the Church of England, banned the Protestant prayerbook issued by King Edward, and then revoked the divorce of her parents. Intolerant of all who opposed her, Mary had hundreds

Elizabeth Tudor was 12 years old when this portrait was painted.

of Protestants burned at the stake in the name of the Catholic church. Eventually, the unrelenting queen became known as "Bloody Mary."

Since Princess Elizabeth—the next in line for the crown—was a Protestant, her life was in constant danger during Mary's reign. She pretended that she had become a Roman Catholic, but Queen Mary never believed her. For a long time, Elizabeth was kept under close watch. Then, when a Protestant rebellion broke out against the queen, Elizabeth was arrested and thrown into the dreaded Tower of London. She insisted that she had played no part in the rebellion, and she was eventually released (Queen Mary was unable to prove her guilt). As a result of this perilous experience, young Elizabeth Tudor learned to be cautious in every situation. She kept her convictions to herself, and she never completely trusted anyone—even those who were closest to her.

In 1554, Queen Mary wed Philip of Spain—her second cousin, and a Catholic like herself. Since Spain had long been an enemy of England, Mary's subjects were strongly opposed to the union. But this mattered little to the self-righteous queen. During their childless marriage, Mary devoted herself to reestablishing Catholicism in England while Philip fought a disastrous war against France. Philip had never really loved the queen (he had married her only for political purposes), and after he lost the war to France, he deserted her.

Mary Tudor died in 1558, after reigning for five dismal, strife-ridden years. Since the 42-year-old queen had no heirs, the throne automatically went to young Elizabeth Tudor. Elizabeth had always been popular among the people, and when she replaced "Bloody Mary" as queen

Mary I, as portrayed by Master John
in 1544

of England, the nation heaved a sigh of relief.

A radiant 25-year-old Elizabeth was crowned queen in Westminster Abbey on January 15, 1559. Dressed in white, crimson, and gold, with her long red hair streaming down her back, the new queen rode through the streets of London amid a tumultuous welcome. "Time!" she cried out to her cheering subjects. "Time has brought me here!" She had waited patiently throughout the long years of hardship and rejection; now, at last, her wait was over.

Elizabeth fell in love with the people, and the people fell in love with her. The love affair continued throughout Elizabeth's long reign. Unlike Queen Mary, who was half Spanish, Queen Elizabeth was 100 percent English—

and proud of it. This, of course, made her all the more popular. Affectionately known as "Good Queen Bess," she was fiercely devoted to her subjects and to her nation. "I care not for myself," she said after her coronation. "My care is for my people."

When Elizabeth inherited the throne, England was in terrible shape. The war against France had just been lost; the royal treasury was all but exhausted; and the question of England's religion was still raging. The machinery of justice had suffered a severe setback during Mary Tudor's bigoted reign, and England's place in the world had fallen. As one chronicler put it, the nation had "many steadfast enemies, but no steadfast friends."

By the end of Elizabeth's reign, England was the wealthiest, most powerful nation in the world. One of the first things Queen Elizabeth did to achieve this goal was to appoint Sir William Cecil as her chief adviser. Cecil held that important position until his death, and he served the queen well. Elizabeth listened carefully to his advice, rarely making a move without him. In the end, however, she alone made all the final decisions. Demanding that Parliament treat her as the ruler of England, Elizabeth once said, "I know I have but the body of a weak and feeble woman, but I have the heart and stomach of a king, and of a king of England, too." On another occasion, the fearless ruler declared, "I may not be a lion, but I have a lion's heart!"

If Queen Elizabeth was proud and courageous, she was also shrewd and intelligent. Elizabeth realized that before she could restore order to her kingdom and present a strong front against her enemies, she would first have to end the religious strife that had begun under Mary

Tudor's reign. So, in 1559, she reestablished the Church of England, making it the official state church. A short time later, she issued an official English prayerbook — a prayerbook that was so ambiguous it could be considered "ours" by Protestants and Catholics alike. In this way, Queen Elizabeth managed to please the Protestants without completely alienating the Catholic minority. The Elizabethan Settlement, as it is called, was one of Elizabeth's greatest accomplishments.

Having restored peace and order to her beloved England, Elizabeth was next faced with the question of marriage. The queen's advisers repeatedly urged her to marry. They feared that if she died without an heir, the throne would go to her Catholic cousin Mary Stuart, Queen of Scots. Queen Elizabeth claimed that she was already "bound in marriage to the realm," but she quieted her advisers by promising to take a husband.

Over the years, dozens of prominent suitors asked for the queen's hand in marriage. Among them were the archduke of Austria, the duke of Anjou (who later became Henry II of France), and even Philip II of Spain — Elizabeth's brother-in-law! Queen Elizabeth didn't reject any of their proposals, but she didn't accept any of them, either. She preferred to play the waiting game, to reap the political advantages of remaining single. Elizabeth knew that as long as she kept the dukes and princes of Europe dangling, she would retain greater bargaining powers with their countries. So, despite all the proposals she received, Elizabeth I never married. By the time of her death, she was known far and wide as the "Virgin Queen."

What kind of woman was Elizabeth Tudor? Far from cold and unfeeling, she was affectionate, fun-loving, and flirtatious. She had her father's bad temper, and it has been said that she "swore like a sailor" when she was angry. But she could also be the perfect lady when the occasion demanded. A pretty woman with red hair, golden-brown eyes, and fair white skin, Queen Elizabeth thrived on flattery. She loved beautiful clothes, and, though otherwise thrifty, she permitted herself a huge and fashionable wardrobe (this was probably her way of compensating for the clothes denied her when she was a girl). She was a sensational dancer, an accomplished scholar, a great sportswoman, and a witty conversationalist. In short, Elizabeth Tudor was the kind of woman most men find exciting and challenging.

Although the "Virgin Queen" never married, she fell in love more than once during her lifetime. Her first and longest romance was with a handsome young man named Robert Dudley. Since Dudley was not only a commoner but also a married man, the affair was doomed from the very beginning. Yet, it lasted for many years.

In 1560, Dudley's long-estranged wife died under mysterious circumstances. Servants found her one Sunday morning at the foot of a staircase, her neck broken. Though no one saw her die, the court ruled that her death was "accidental" (most historians believe it was suicide). At first, it seemed that this was the opening Dudley and Elizabeth had been waiting for, the stroke of fate that would allow them to marry. But when Elizabeth learned that her subjects believed Dudley had *killed his wife* to marry her, she steered away from making any hasty moves. Her worst fear was that if she married Dudley, she would create an even greater scandal. So she put him off. Indefinitely.

Robert Dudley

Dudley was a much weaker person than Elizabeth, and he grew impatient with her. Finally, he remarried. Elizabeth was enraged at first, but she eventually forgave Dudley, even going so far as to make him earl of Leicester. The fact that Elizabeth and Dudley remained close friends gave rise to much gossip. While some people believed that Dudley was merely the queen's admirer and constant companion, others were convinced that the couple were lovers.

Whatever the case, Elizabeth's one great regret was that she never had a child. She knew that when she died, there would be no one to carry on the reign of the Tudors. Worse yet, the throne would probably go to her cousin Mary Stuart, a devout Roman Catholic. When Mary, Queen of Scots, gave birth to a son in 1566, Elizabeth was both envious and alarmed. Now that her ambitious young cousin had a male heir, her claim to the English throne seemed all the more secure—and all the more foreboding.

Over the years, Mary Stuart became involved in a number of plots against Elizabeth. The Catholic queen first came to England in 1568, after her Protestant subjects forced her to abdicate the Scottish throne. Once in England, Mary became the willing tool of power-hungry rebels, most of them Roman Catholic. Their goal was to seize the throne from Elizabeth and to make Mary queen.

After Queen Elizabeth was excommunicated from the Roman Catholic church in 1570, Mary Stuart and her supporters dredged up the question of Elizabeth's legitimacy. Claiming that she was born out of wedlock, they said she had no right to be England's ruler. The rightful ruler of England was Mary Stuart, they said, not Elizabeth.

In the face of these attacks, Queen Elizabeth had security tightened around her cousin, keeping her prisoner in a series of castles. But the plots kept unwinding. Elizabeth's advisers urged her to order Mary's execution, but Elizabeth tolerated her cousin's treacherous deeds for almost 20 years. Then, in 1587, her patience was finally tried beyond endurance. Learning of Mary Stuart's involvement in a plot to kill her, Queen Elizabeth signed the warrant for her cousin's execution. Most Englishmen celebrated Mary Stuart's death, but Queen Elizabeth wept bitter tears over it. Perhaps she felt that her victory over Mary was really a defeat. After all, in losing Mary Stuart, she lost one of her last close relatives.

A year after her treacherous cousin was beheaded, Queen Elizabeth faced an even greater enemy — Catholic Spain. Tensions had been mounting between the two rival powers for a long time. While Spanish colonizers were busy settling their vast holdings in the New World,

English explorers were busy raiding Spanish galleons and taking over Spanish trade routes. To Philip II of Spain, this was an intolerable situation. Finally, in 1588, Spain's ruler decided to strike back at England. With his "Invincible Armada" of 130 warships, he set sail for Queen Elizabeth's island kingdom. Philip's aim was simple: he would crush Elizabeth's forces, proclaim himself king, and then reestablish the Catholic church in England.

When she learned of Philip's intentions, Queen Elizabeth quickly assessed her strength. A lesser ruler would have been discouraged, for England had no standing army at the time (Elizabeth had always dismissed her troops in times of peace). England had a strong and experienced navy, but it was only about half the size of the Spanish Armada. Still, Elizabeth I was confident of her country's ability to defend itself against Spain. England's warships were smaller than those of Spain, and fewer in number, but they were faster, lighter, and better able to attack and retreat quickly. So, too, England had a large reservoir of skilled sailors to draw from. After gaining the support of such daring sea captains as Sir Francis Drake and Sir John Hawkins, Queen Elizabeth made Admiral Lord Charles Howard commander-in-chief of the English fleet. Then she hastily put together an army, appointing her long-time friend Robert Dudley as lieutenant general of the armed forces.

As the mighty Spanish Armada neared her homeland, Queen Elizabeth visited her troops at a place called Tilbury. Dressed in full armor and mounted on a horse, she swore her undying loyalty to England. "I have always placed my strength in the loyal hearts of my subjects," the queen said. "I am resolved to live or die among you,

This engraving depicts a dramatic moment during the defeat of the Spanish Armada.

to lay down for God, for my kingdom, and for my people, my honor and my blood, even in the dust." With these words, Good Queen Bess rallied the troops behind her.

On July 30, 1588, the Spanish Armada entered the English Channel. Not since the Norman Conquest, back in the 11th century, had England been invaded. The English forces were greatly outnumbered, having only 80 ships to Spain's 130. Yet, they were determined to defend their homeland, and they fought much harder than their enemies. After driving the Spanish Armada out of the English Channel and then chasing it for eight more days, the English fleet finally forced its enemy into battle.

The English fought valiantly, sinking several Spanish
ships and inflicting heavy damage on scores of others.
Broken by the fierce attack, the Spanish Armada fled for
home. Violent storms in the North Sea destroyed much
of the fleet, and only 67 of the original 130 warships
managed to reach Spain.

Safe once again, all of England was delirious with joy,
united in pride. Queen Elizabeth had gambled on the
loyalty of her people, and she had scored a brilliant
victory. With the defeat of the Spanish Armada, England
established itself as a major naval power and took up its
place as "Mistress of the Seas." In defiance of Spain,

England now went about the task of establishing its own empire in the New World—an empire that would one day make England the wealthiest nation in the world.

The final years of Elizabeth's reign were golden ones for England. They were years of exploration and discovery, of trade and expansion, of peace and prosperity. While some daring adventurers roamed the seas in search of new lands and new sea routes, others formed great trade companies, such as the East India Company. Still others explored the coasts of North and South America, establishing English colonies in the New World. One of the first of these colonies was founded by Sir Walter Raleigh in what is now the eastern United States. Raleigh named the colony "Virginia," in honor of Elizabeth, the "Virgin Queen."

This golden age in English history was also a period of genius and creativity, a period marked by the achievements of many great scholars, musicians, poets, and dramatists. Edmund Spenser, Francis Bacon, Christopher Marlowe, Ben Jonson—these were but a few of the outstanding writers who lived during the reign of Queen Elizabeth. And towering above them all was William Shakespeare, the greatest dramatist the world has ever known.

These years of unmatched achievement were indeed "golden" years for England, but they were lonely years for Queen Elizabeth. Robert Dudley had died of a fever in 1588, while leading English troops against the invading forces of Spain. Overwhelmed by Dudley's death, Elizabeth saved his last letters for years, and wept as she reread them. The Virgin Queen was growing old by now, and she realized that her looks were fading. In a vain

Sir Walter Raleigh

William Shakespeare

attempt to turn back the clock, she began wearing gaudy red wigs and thick, chalky makeup. When she finally realized that nothing could restore her youthful appearance, the queen ordered that every mirror in her palace be removed.

Despite her withering appearance, Queen Elizabeth never lacked for male companionship. Nor did she lack for romance. When 21-year-old Robert Devereux, earl of Essex, began courting her, the queen became infatuated with him. Devereux was handsome, charming, hot-blooded, courageous—many of the things Elizabeth liked in a man. Even more important, he made the aging queen feel young again.

Elizabeth doted on her handsome suitor, but not to the point of making a fool of herself. After all, she was a queen, and Devereux a mere earl. During the course of their long and sometimes stormy romance, Devereux more than once made known his desire to marry the queen and sit beside her on the throne. But Elizabeth would have none of it. She loved Devereux and did not want to lose him, but she was not about to share her throne with him — even if this meant losing him forever.

When the ambitious earl of Essex finally realized that Queen Elizabeth would never marry him, he became bitter and resentful. He would gain control of the throne, he vowed, no matter what the cost. In 1601, Devereux tried to make good his vow. Marching toward the royal palace with only a handful of supporters, he made a foolhardy attempt to overthrow the queen. The rebellion failed, and Devereux was imprisoned in the Tower of London. Elizabeth did not hesitate to sign his death warrant. "He has at last revealed what was long on his mind," she said impassively. Hours later, Devereux was beheaded. So ended the last of Queen Elizabeth's ill-fated romances.

Elizabeth was tired now, and more lonely than she had ever been before. Even her beloved friend and adviser William Cecil had died. (Elizabeth had sat at his bedside on the night of his death, holding his hand until the end.) Queen Elizabeth had accomplished much during her long and vigorous reign; now, she was ready to die, ready to leave behind the cares of the world and let another ruler take her place on the throne.

In January of 1603 — less than two years after Robert Devereux was beheaded — Queen Elizabeth fell ill with a cold and fever. Instead of going to bed, as her doctors ordered, the dying queen carried out the task of putting her affairs in order. Her successor, she decided, would be

James Stuart, the son of Mary, Queen of Scots. In addition to being one of her last remaining relatives, James was a Protestant—a strong point in his favor. Had he been a Catholic (like his mother), Queen Elizabeth never would have named him as her successor.

Knowing that the end was near, Elizabeth sent for the archbishop of Canterbury so that he might prepare her for death. Then, on the mild spring morning of March 24, 1603, Elizabeth Tudor died in her sleep. The 69-year-old queen had ruled England for 45 years, and she had become a legend in her own time—loved by England, respected by the world. With her death, one of the most glorious periods in English history came to an end. This period would be forever known as the Elizabethan Age, after the ruler who had made it great.

An unfinished portrait of Marie Antoinette at age 36, by A. Kucharski

Marie Antoinette (1755-1793)
They Called Her "Madame Deficit"

In the end, she finally understood why the people had turned against her. She understood why they no longer cheered her, and why they wanted to see her disgraced. But by then, it was too late. There was nothing left for her to do but wait, ill and alone, in her small dingy cell.

They had taken everything away from her. First her friends, then her husband, and finally her children. They had even taken the little gold watch her mother had given her 24 years before, when she left her homeland of Austria for the first time. Then, she had been a storybook princess with everything to live for—even her own prince charming. She would marry her prince one day, but she would not live "happily ever after." Hers was a story with a much darker ending.

Who was this tragic woman? History remembers her as the beautiful, fun-loving bride of a king who was too weak to turn back the tides of revolution. History remembers her as "Madame Deficit," a proud and extravagant ruler who failed to respond to the needs of her people at a time when their needs were great. History remembers her as Marie Antoinette, the ill-fated queen of France who died on the guillotine during the French Revolution.

Born in Austria on November 2, 1755, Marie Antoinette was the youngest daughter of Empress Maria Theresa and Emperor Francis I, co-rulers of the Holy Roman Empire. When Princess Marie was 10 years old, her father died, leaving her mother with an empire to govern and with eight children to raise. Empress Maria quickly mastered the art of statesmanship, and she was recognized throughout Europe as a shrewd and able ruler. A practical parent as well, she arranged politically profitable marriages for her sons and daughters when they were still playing with toy soldiers and china dolls. For Marie Antoinette, her youngest daughter, the empress arranged the best match of all. Princess Marie would marry Prince Louis—the grandson of King Louis XV, and the heir to the throne of France. When his turn came, Louis would reign over the most beautiful country in Europe. And at his side would be Marie Antoinette, queen of France.

The princess who was raised to become queen was a lively, carefree child who found life delightful. Young Marie Antoinette was not pretty in the classical sense, but there were many who considered her beautiful. She had clear, delicate skin, long silky hair, and the unmistakable poise and grace of a queen. Her dark-blue eyes were perhaps her most outstanding feature. Sparkling and alert, they seemed to reflect her vitality, her love of life. (Years later, Marie Antoinette's enemies would describe her eyes as "bold" and "insolent.")

Partly because she was her mother's favorite, Marie Antoinette was allowed to get by with a lot more mischief than her older brothers and sisters. Daily studies were a

Empress Maria Theresa, by the artist Van der Meytens

Marie Antoinette, at age 13; artist unknown

part of her official schedule, but when the self-willed little princess played hooky, no one disciplined her. Everyone, it seems, doted on her, giving her all that her heart desired. Is it any wonder, then, that Marie Antoinette grew up believing she would always be able to charm everyone she met?

In 1769, when Marie Antoinette was 14 years old, her betrothal to Prince Louis of France became official. One year later it was decided that she should journey to France to meet her future husband and to prepare for her eventual role as queen. For several weeks before leaving Austria, Princess Marie slept with her mother every night—something she hadn't done since earliest childhood. Looking at the sleeping princess, Empress Maria would often worry. Had she given her daughter the right kind of upbringing? She was so frivolous, so sheltered, so used to having her own way. The empress could only pray that her daughter would be able to cope with life, and never be hurt or disappointed.

The year was 1770, and Marie Antoinette was barely 15 years old. Outfitted in satin and jewels, the radiant bride-to-be set out for France, leaving her homeland forever. Despite her tears, Marie Antoinette was eager to begin the adventure ahead, and confident that she would be admired and adored in France. After accepting a little gold watch from her mother, she kissed the empress goodbye. This was to be the last time they would ever see each other.

Marie Antoinette's debut in France was an outstanding success. Old King Louis XV, Prince Louis's grandfather, had always appreciated lovely women. Now, upon meeting Marie Antoinette for the first time, he congratulated himself on the excellent choice he had made for his grandson. The king's advisers and courtiers were just as impressed with the newly arrived princess, and they showered her with compliments. But Prince Louis—a shy, awkward boy of 16—hung back. In fact, he had to be pushed and prodded into giving his betrothed a formal kiss of welcome! Throughout their marriage, Louis would always be in awe of his stunning wife, ready to give in to her every whim in order to win her gratitude and avoid her disdain.

A clumsy, dull-witted youth whose main pleasure in life was eating, Prince Louis was something less than a prince charming. But if Marie Antoinette was disappointed with her future husband, she didn't show it. Marriage plans proceeded smoothly, and elaborate public festivities were scheduled to follow the wedding. This would give the common people of France their first chance to meet Marie Antoinette, their future queen. It would also help them to forget about the drudgery of their lives—and about the high taxes they were paying to support the French monarchy.

The marriage of Marie Antoinette and Prince Louis took place on May 16, 1770. Dressed in silver and gold, the radiant bride was cheered and greeted by thousands of adoring well-wishers as she and Louis rode through the streets of Paris. Then, as a climax to the wedding, a dazzling fireworks display was held. Pandemonium broke out when a water-seller's cart was overturned, and many people were trampled to death. Yet, even as the bodies were being laid out for identification, the royal festivities continued. Some people believed that the disaster was a bad omen, a sign that the reign of Louis and Marie Antoinette would be marked with tragedy.

After the wedding, 15-year-old Marie Antoinette settled down to life at the French court, in the luxurious palace of Versailles. While her public life was exciting, her private life was empty and unfulfilling. Prince Louis was a reluctant husband who showed his young wife little warmth or understanding. Many nights, he would wolf down his evening meal and then fall asleep in his chair. Apparently, he found life very uneventful. "Nothing happened today," he often wrote in his diary, even when his world was crashing down on him.

Undaunted by her husband's apathy, and eager to live life to the hilt, Marie Antoinette gathered around her a circle of fun-loving young people. The group included Prince Louis's two younger brothers, Provence and Artois; his cousin Phillippe Egalite; and, later, his younger

Marie Antoinette with her maids of honor, by Gautier-Dagoty

sister, Princess Elisabeth. The youths often went about their merrymaking in the palace itself, dancing, gambling, and enacting plays that made fun of Prince Louis. Even more daring were their escapades to Paris ballrooms, where they disguised themselves with masks and danced until dawn. To the great amusement of her friends, Marie Antoinette frequently set Prince Louis's clock ahead so that he would doze off earlier than usual, thus allowing Marie and her friends more time for fun and games.

In 1774, just four years after Marie Antoinette and Prince Louis were married, King Louis XV died suddenly of smallpox. When notified of the king's death, Louis and Marie shared a single thought: "We are not ready to rule! We are too young!" They were 20 and 19, respectively. In different ways, each was grievously unprepared for the responsibility of ruling France—a nation beset with internal crises and a restless populace. Yet, in June of 1774, Louis was crowned King Louis XVI, and Marie Antoinette became queen of France.

Despite her frivolous behavior and her extravagant tastes, Marie Antoinette was extremely popular during the first few years of her reign. It was almost as if *she* were the real monarch, and Louis her mere companion. The people wildly applauded the queen's frequent appearances in Paris, and all of Europe raved about her beauty and charm. A fashion-setter in both clothes and hairdos, Marie Antoinette was the darling of jewelers, dress-makers, and hair stylists alike. Understandably enough, this segment of French society remained loyal to the queen far beyond the time when most working people were clamoring for her downfall.

Marie Antoinette gave up her jewel-trimmed gowns and elaborate hairdos in favor of a simple "country girl" look when she and King Louis moved into the Petit Trianon, a small country house near the palace of Versailles. Life in the old palace had been too stiff and formal for the high-spirited queen, and she had often complained of living in a "fishbowl," forever surrounded by courtiers and servants. Once she moved into the Petit Trianon, the queen enjoyed more privacy and freedom, and simplicity became her goal. Ironically, however, it cost a fortune to create the simplicity at the Petit Trianon. The building itself was completely redecorated, and Marie Antoinette's entire wardrobe was replaced to give the queen the informal look of a milkmaid. As it happened, some of the

After she tired of life in the palace, Marie Antoinette moved into the Petit Trianon, shown above.

"simple" straw hats designed for the queen cost more than a French working man made in a year.

In addition to her roles as a queen and a fashion-setter, Marie Antoinette assumed the role of a mother. Between 1778 and 1786, four children were born to her and King Louis. Only two of them survived early childhood. They were Marie Therese, born in 1778; and the dauphin, or crown prince, Louis, born in 1785. From most accounts, Marie Antoinette appears to have been an affectionate mother who enjoyed playing with children. Yet, she frequently entrusted them to others so that she could keep up her busy social life. Nothing, it seems, held the queen's attention for very long.

In his patient, bumbling way, King Louis put up with

This idyllic hamlet was yet another of the French queen's homes away from the palace.

his wife's capricious behavior and continued to indulge all her whims—even when they affected statesmanship. The queen insisted that her friends get choice court appointments at outrageous salaries, and she constantly overspent her more-than-generous allowance. As Marie Antoinette's extravagance went unchecked, the royal treasury teetered on bankruptcy. This, in turn, led to higher taxes for the already-overtaxed working people of France. When the king's advisers at last insisted that the royal budget be reduced, the queen urged her husband to dismiss them.

Marie Antoinette was fast becoming France's greatest liability. The people had a new name for her now; they called her "Madame Deficit." No longer did they cheer themselves hoarse when she rode through the streets of Paris. No longer did they overlook her shortcomings simply because she was young and beautiful, an international showpiece. The people were being shortchanged, and they intended to let the queen know it.

The unrest in France was stimulated, in part, by the demand of the American colonies for freedom from British oppression. Revolution was in the air, and liberty and equality were more than idealistic words. The French people were tired of supporting a government that gave them nothing but high taxes and wars they did not want. They might have forgiven King Louis had he seemed to really care about them, but his words and actions suggested otherwise. When the common people asked for lower taxes and other reforms, the king brushed their requests aside, calling them "unthinkable." The people could only conclude that King Louis was being influenced and manipulated by "that foreigner," his wife.

Marie Antoinette with two of her children

Louis XVI, as portrayed by Du Plessis

To a great extent, the people were right. King Louis XVI was no tyrant, but he was weak and indecisive. And rather than giving him the kind of support he needed, Marie Antoinette taunted him for his weakness, urging him to be strong instead of wise. When King Louis took his wife's advice and ignored the demands of his people, he brought France that much closer to a revolution.

It is easy to point out Marie Antoinette's faults, particularly her extravagance and poor judgment. But it should be remembered that she was not equipped, either by education or by temperament, to understand and grapple with national problems. The mood of the French people, the drudgery of their lives, their complaints and their demands—all of these things were alien to her. Like many rulers, Marie Antoinette believed that those at the top could do no wrong, that they were immune from the criticism of the masses. So, while hatred and division swirled around her, she retreated into her own private world, confident that the storm would soon pass.

When told that the common people of France were without bread, did Marie Antoinette really say: "Then let them eat cake"? Most historians think not. But this and other stories about the arrogant queen were widely believed, and they contributed to her downfall. As the public's hatred of Marie Antoinette—and of all she stood for—intensified, the cries for a revolution grew louder. A number of leaders emerged before long, and the angry common people of France rallied behind them. Their goals were to overthrow the monarchy and to wipe out the class divisions in France.

Once the French Revolution got under way, things happened quickly. On July 14, 1789, the citizens of Paris took up arms and stormed the Bastille, a mighty fortress-prison. They killed the prison governor, released all the prisoners (most of whom were enemies of the monarchy), and seized over 30,000 muskets. In the days and weeks that followed, many French noblemen fled to England and to other countries, fearing the wrath of the revolutionists. Those who did not leave were arrested and imprisoned. As the French Revolution gained momentum, thousands of political prisoners died on the guillotine, a machine for beheading. This massacre signaled the beginning of the Reign of Terror, which continued until the French Revolution ended in 1794.

The time was October of 1789. Nearly all of Marie Antoinette's friends had deserted her, and the future looked grim. But rather than escape from France and save herself, Marie Antoinette chose to remain by her husband's side. On October 5, 1789, the inevitable happened: an angry Paris mob marched to Versailles and captured the royal family. Louis XVI, Marie Antoinette, and their two children were brought to Paris the next day, and imprisoned in Tuileries Palace. "We have the baker, the baker's wife, and the baker's son!" shouted the revolutionists. "Now we will have bread!"

The king and queen were held captive in Tuileries Palace for almost two years. They were not treated badly, and they lived in comparative comfort. With them were their children, a number of their favorite servants, and Princess Elisabeth, the king's sister. Marie Antoinette probably spent more time with her children during this period of imprisonment than she ever had before. Partly for her children's sake, she put up a convincing show of strength and courage.

On June 20, 1791, the royal family made a dramatic attempt at escape, fleeing from Paris in the middle of the night. They were caught early the next morning, however, and were brought back to Tuileries Palace. A short time later, the royal family was moved to a grim Paris building called the Temple. King Louis stubbornly refused to give in to the demands of the revolutionists, and he was put on trial in January of 1793. Somehow, Louis had never really believed that his subjects would overthrow him; when at last they condemned him to death, he was genuinely shocked.

The night before his execution, Louis XVI was allowed to spend two hours with his family. It was a tearful, emotional scene. After the king left, Marie Antoinette spent the long night listening in anguish as her little gold watch ticked away the last hours of her husband's life.

Imprisoned in the Temple, the royal family dines under the watchful eyes of their keepers.

When the bells of Paris rang out the next morning, the queen knew that her husband was dead.

The death of King Louis, and the deaths of thousands of French noblemen, did not satisfy the revolutionists. The real culprit was the queen, they reasoned, the one person who best symbolized the extravagance and corruption of the French monarchy. "Kill the Austrian!" demanded Marie Antoinette's enemies. "Kill the foreigner!" Those who would have shown the queen some mercy remained silent.

Marie Antoinette remained in the Temple with her children and Princess Elisabeth for several weeks after King Louis's death. Then, without warning, three men came one night to take her son, the dauphin Louis. The queen clung to her child, crying that the men would have to kill her first before they could take him away. But the men easily separated young Louis from his mother, taking him to quarters on another floor of the Temple.

Days later, Marie Antoinette was moved from the Temple to a small dingy room in the Conciergerie, or the common prison. The queen was kept under constant guard, and she was not permitted any privacy, even to dress and undress. The only kindness allowed her was the companionship of a young servant girl named Rosalie. The queen's precious gold watch was taken away from her, and she was left with only one white dress, one black dress, and a few pieces of underclothing. Rosalie smuggled in some personal things, however, such as a comb and powder.

The days were long and desolate. Marie Antoinette asked for needles so that she could do needlework, but she was refused them. In desperation, she plucked strings from the ragged curtains in her cell and made a crude kind of lace. She was allowed one or two books, and even though she had never been an avid reader, she read them over and over. Most of the time, however, she sat staring at her hands, nervously switching her wedding ring from one finger to the other.

Marie Antoinette, the once-glamorous queen of France —the woman who had everything—was now without hope, consolation, or even dignity. She was not yet 38 years old, but her hair had already turned white. Her once-sparkling eyes were now sunken and lifeless, and her fair skin was deathly pale. The queen was sick, and when the time came for her trial, there were many who doubted that she could withstand the ordeal. She bore up surprisingly well, however, giving such skillful answers to the judges' questions that some spectators thought she would actually be acquitted. But the judges had made up their minds before the trial began, and Marie Antoinette was pronounced guilty late in the afternoon of October 15, 1793. She was to die on the guillotine before noon the next day.

Marie Antoinette spent her last evening writing a long letter to her sister-in-law, Princess Elisabeth. The letter mainly concerned her children, but in it, the queen also spoke of her personal feelings. She said that she was "innocent" of any wrongdoing, that she had lived only for her family. "I would like to ask pardon for whatever distress I have caused without wishing to do so," she wrote. The queen indicated that she was ready to die, and she asked Elisabeth to be a mother to her children. Unfortunately, the letter never reached Elisabeth, for the French princess was put to death by the revolutionists. Historians disagree on what happened to the dauphin Louis, but it is generally believed that he was murdered by his captors.

Marie Antoinette rose at dawn on the morning of her execution. She had not slept at all, and Rosalie had heard her sobbing throughout the night. Without her watch, the queen did not know how much time was left. She knew only that time was running out. With Rosalie's help, she dressed carefully in a change of underclothing and her white dress. The guards watched her every move, and at one point, the queen cried out: "In the name of God and decency, I beg you give me some privacy!" The guards turned away, their eyes cast to the ground.

Finally, the queen's executioner and four men dressed

The artist Jacques-Louis David drew this pen-portrait of Marie Antoinette during the final hours of her life.

in black came to escort Marie Antoinette to the guillotine. Rosalie had arranged the queen's long white hair neatly, but the executioner pulled out a pair of scissors and slashed it off. He put the hair in his pocket, saving it as a trophy. The queen remained calm and courageous throughout the ordeal, but when she saw that she was to ride to her execution in a cattle cart, she let out a cry of despair. King Louis had at least been allowed the dignity of a coach.

The streets of Paris were lined with mobs of angry, jeering people. At first, the queen stared straight ahead.

Then something made her look at the faces of the people —the once-adoring subjects who had lined these same streets so many times before. Marie Antoinette now saw only hate in their eyes. At one point a child, raised up by his mother for a better view, innocently blew the queen a kiss. Seeing this, Marie Antoinette managed a faint smile.

The guillotine was stationed at the Place de la Revolution, near Tuileries Palace. When they reached it, Marie Antoinette stepped out of the cart unaided, and courageously mounted the platform. She was in such a hurry that she accidentally stepped on the executioner's hand.

"Pardon me, monsieur," she said. "I did not do it on purpose." These were Marie Antoinette's final words. Moments later, the steel blade glistened and fell.

Catherine the Great, 1770

Catherine the Great (1729-1796)
Star of the North

Slender as a reed, pale, and ordinary looking, 14-year-old Princess Sophia Augusta Fredericka of Anhalt-Zerbst was a nobody. She was a German princess, but in name only; her parents were without power, wealth, or prestige. Yet, before her life was over, the obscure German princess would become known throughout Europe as Catherine the Great, empress of all Russia. Along with Queen Elizabeth I of England, she would go down in history as one of the most powerful women ever to sit upon a throne.

The brown-haired, blue-eyed Princess Sophia was born in Stettin, Prussia, on May 2, 1729. She was the only daughter of Christian Augustus of Anhalt-Zerbst—a minor German prince—and Johanna Elizabeth, an impoverished member of the great Romanov family of Russia. Young Princess Sophia lacked beauty and wealth, but she was intelligent, well educated, and self-reliant. An unusually mature girl who enjoyed the company of adults, the princess was much admired by her father for her quick mind and her model behavior. Prince Christian was a devout Lutheran, and he personally saw to his daughter's religious training. More than once, he voiced his hope that Princess Sophia would enter an abbey and devote her life to God.

Unfortunately, Prince Christian died when his daughter was still quite young, leaving her in the hands of her ill-tempered, self-seeking mother. Johanna Elizabeth had never wanted a daughter, and she made no attempt to hide the fact from Princess Sophia. Not unlike the wicked stepmother in "Cinderella," she treated her daughter cruelly, yelling at her often and denying her much. Yet, when the opportunity arose, Johanna Elizabeth did not hesitate to use her daughter to better her own position. A willing if helpless pawn, Princess Sophia did as her mother directed.

The fairy godmother in this cast of 18th-century characters was Elizabeth Romanov—the beautiful, never-wed empress of Russia. For a long time, the empress had been seeking a wife for her nephew, Grand Duke Peter. Peter was Elizabeth's heir to the throne, and whoever married him would rule Russia beside him. In January of 1744, Empress Elizabeth wrote a letter to Johanna Elizabeth, inviting her and her daughter to come to Russia for a visit. Guessing that the empress was considering Princess Sophia as a mate for her nephew, Johanna Elizabeth eagerly accepted the invitation. Fourteen-year-old Princess Sophia had inherited her mother's ambition, and she prayed that Empress Elizabeth would accept her as a bride for the grand duke. "Child as I was," she later wrote, "the title of queen caressed my ears. . . ."

This 18th-century engraving shows what St. Petersburg looked like when Catherine first arrived there.

The trip to Russia was an ordeal that lasted for over six weeks. Accompanied by her nagging mother, and shivering from the cold, young Princess Sophia at last arrived in St. Petersburg (now Leningrad), home of the Winter Palace. To her disappointment, the German princess was greeted with little fanfare or warmth at the Russian court. And adding to the frigid reception was a remark made by Grand Duke Peter, an ugly, dull-witted youth of 15. Claiming that he wanted to marry "someone else," he said that he wished Princess Sophia "would go away."

In no position to be as candid as the grand duke, Princess Sophia concealed her distaste for the ungainly boy and tried to be friendly. And, displaying model behavior, she was properly humble and respectful in the presence of Empress Elizabeth. Since the princess was forthright by nature, she must have cringed inwardly as she played the role of mock servility. She played the role well, however, and the rewards were quick in coming. Impressed with the princess's good breeding and keen mind, Empress Elizabeth took an immediate liking to her. Before long, the empress began to trust the teen-age princess of Anhalt-Zerbst more than she trusted her own blood relatives!

So that she might win the empress's total approval, Princess Sophia adopted Russia as her own country. Then she undertook the task of transforming herself into a good Russian. She studied the complicated language and history of Russia, and she took instructions in the Greek Orthodox religion, the official religion of Russia. Although the industrious young princess learned the ways of Russia in record time, she did so at the cost of her health. She pushed herself too hard—even to the point of study-ing through the night—and she at last became seriously ill. After a short period of bed rest, however, Princess Sophia recovered completely.

On June 29, 1744, some five months after her arrival in St. Petersburg, Princess Sophia was received into the Greek Orthodox church. It was on this day that her name was officially changed from Sophia Augusta Fredericka to Catherine Alexeievna, the Russian name Empress Elizabeth had picked for her. June 29, 1744, was also the day of young Catherine's betrothal to Grand Duke Peter. The German princess had worked hard for this important day, and now she delighted in it.

This portrait of Peter and Catherine was painted by G. C. Groot in 1744, around the time of their betrothal.

A year after her betrothal, 16-year-old Catherine Alexeievna married Grand Duke Peter, thus gaining the title of "grand duchess." Clearly, Catherine had married for power, not for love. "I did not care about Peter," she wrote in her diary, "but I did care about the crown." Seven years later, Grand Duchess Catherine claimed that her marriage to Peter still had not been consummated. Catherine had taken many lovers by this time, however, and she was well versed in the ways of love. Sensual and intelligent, she charmed and seduced every man she wanted. Men became her pawns, useful only so long as they could bring her pleasure or aid her in her calculated climb to the throne.

Grand Duke Peter openly despised his power-hungry wife, and he did not meddle in her affairs. Nor did he bother to prepare himself for his eventual role as emperor of Russia. Instead, he spent his days playing cards, studying ships, and training dogs and monkeys. His two favorite pastimes were practicing the violin and playing with his tin soldiers (he had several thousand of them). The grand duke had a weakness for wine, and he drank to excess. More often than not, this made him feel lusty and amorous. But rather than turn to his despised wife, Peter spent his evenings fraternizing with his servants.

Whereas the pleasure-loving Peter cared little about Russia, his wife was more fervently patriotic than most full-blooded Russians. Catherine had resolved to become "a good Russian," and she had succeeded in this. When she was not thinking about her beloved Russia, she was thinking about the throne—and about how she would one day seize it for herself. To prepare herself for that day, Catherine learned the ways of statecraft and political intrigue from the aging Empress Elizabeth. The empress had long worried about leaving the throne to Peter (she called him an "imbecile"), and she was pleased that Catherine was taking such an active interest in affairs of state. When Peter assumed the throne, thought the empress, Catherine would be there to guide him.

As the years passed, Catherine's thirst for knowledge intensified. She devoured every book she could find on statecraft, and she became familiar with the works of such brilliant philosophers as Diderot and Voltaire. Disciples of the Age of Reason, these men attacked ignorance, superstition, cruelty, and social injustice—the very evils that Catherine saw everywhere in Russia. At the time, Russia was a semiprimitive, almost barbarian, country. Catherine vowed that when she became empress, she would replace ignorance with knowledge, injustice with justice. More important, she would bring to Russia the culture and civilization of the West. This, Catherine mused, would be her legacy to Russia.

In 1754, Catherine took time out from her studies to give birth to a son, christened Paul. The child was not Peter's, but the grand duke never knew this. As for Empress Elizabeth, she embraced the child as her own, all but wrenching him from his mother's arms. Catherine did not want to risk incurring the empress's wrath, so she said nothing. Before long, then, Empress Elizabeth virtually replaced Catherine as the boy's mother.

With Empress Elizabeth bringing up her son, with her estranged husband actively avoiding her, and with her ill-tempered mother finally leaving Russia in a huff, 25-year-old Catherine Alexeievna was left more and more on her own. This was much to Catherine's liking, for now she had more time to devote to her studies. Equally important, the shrewd grand duchess now had more time to cultivate the friendship of powerful and important men —men who might help her to become empress one day.

Five such men were the Orlov brothers, all of them high-ranking officers of the royal guard. Catherine won them over completely, and they took up her cause as their own. Now, all Catherine had to do was to bide her time. Once the aged Empress Elizabeth died, Catherine and her supporters would make their move. They would move quickly, they decided, and with thunderous force.

As Catherine grew bolder in her quest for power, she grew brasher in her quest for romance, moving from one partner to another. When the grand duchess's love life at last became a topic of court gossip, Grand Duke Peter threatened Catherine with a divorce. Empress Elizabeth would not hear of such a thing, however. She reminded Peter of his own sordid affairs, and then told him that she would disinherit him if he went through with the divorce. Knowing that his aunt rarely made empty threats, Peter sheepishly retreated. Yet, in the years that followed, he took to publicly insulting Catherine whenever the occasion allowed. As if immune to her husband's attacks, Catherine simply laughed them off. Her day would come soon enough, she told herself. She would have her revenge.

On Christmas Day, 1761, Empress Elizabeth died, leaving the thone to her witless nephew. Peter, who became Emperor Peter III in January of 1762, was only 33 years old at the time; his wife, Catherine, was but 32. In less than a year, the industrious foreigner would wrest the crown from her husband and become empress of all

Russia. Before she acted, however, she would allow Peter to put the noose around his own neck—something the incompetent ruler would do in short order.

To no one's surprise—least of all Catherine's—Peter proved himself to be a pitifully ineffective ruler. He flaunted his private affairs, groveled before foreign monarchs, usurped the wealth of the church, and engaged Russia in a foolhardy and unpopular war against Denmark. Achieving this dismal record in a mere six months, Peter III lost the respect of the people and so sealed his doom. While the hapless emperor guzzled down his wine and played merrily on his fiddle, the shrewd Catherine drew new supporters into her plot to overthrow her husband and to seize the throne for herself.

On June 28, 1762, while Peter was away from St. Petersburg on a pleasure trip, the moment Catherine had been waiting for finally arrived. Backed by the royal guard, the Russian nobility, and the Greek Orthodox church, Catherine marched from Peterhof Palace, a country house, to St. Petersburg, 19 miles away. In the bloodless revolution that followed, she seized the throne and proclaimed herself ruler of Russia. The 33-year-old Catherine was crowned empress that same day. Hours later, when she appeared on the balcony of the Winter Palace, the radiant empress was cheered by nearly all of St. Petersburg. "Long live the empress!" shouted her subjects. "Long live Catherine, Little Mother of Russia!"

Before leaving the balcony, Catherine spoke to the cheering crowds. "We have seen Ourselves obliged," she said, "with the help of God and his Justice, and in response to the wishes of Our subjects, to ascend the throne as Catherine II, Empress and Autocrat of all the Russians.

Catherine II, Little Mother of Russia

In turn, Our faithful subjects have taken the solemn oath of allegiance to Us." With this, the empress opened the doors of the Winter Palace, allowing the people to kneel at her feet and to kiss her hand. Catherine's place on the throne was thus secure, with all of St. Petersburg in the palm of her hand.

Meanwhile, Peter was hunted down and imprisoned in the palace of Ropsha, a country house outside of St. Petersburg. On June 29, 1762, the bewildered emperor was forced to abdicate the throne to his wife, the empress. Seven days later, on July 6, Peter was murdered by one of Catherine's most loyal supporters. When she announced her husband's death the next day, Catherine said only that it had "pleased Almighty God to remove the late emperor by a sudden and violent malady." In all the years that followed, Catherine never again spoke of her husband's death. Nor did her subjects ever question her about it. Catherine was empress of Russia, and that was all that mattered.

Influenced by the liberal ideas of Voltaire and other French philosophers, Catherine II set out to become a model ruler, a benevolent "mother" to her people. For a time, at least, it seemed as if she might actually succeed in this. Unlike the rulers before her, Catherine spoke of freedom and justice and equality. One day, she promised, she would abolish the oppressive institution of serfdom, freeing the peasants of Russia from their all-powerful masters, the nobles. All her subjects would be equal in the eyes of the law, she continued, and all would have a voice in the government.

With promises such as these, Catherine II won the love of the peasants and the praise of the philosophers, who called her a "champion of the people" and who hailed her as the "Star of the North." In 1767, Catherine even went so far as to draw up some sweeping charters for reform, the most controversial charter calling for the gradual elimination of serfdom. But when the liberal-minded empress came up against the strong resistance of the

Russian nobility, she quickly retreated. The nobles had helped Catherine become empress, and she feared that they would turn against her if she proceeded with her plans to free the serfs and to limit the powers of the nobles. So, abandoning her humanitarian ideals, Catherine II buckled under the pressure of the nobility.

In the years that followed, Catherine continued to talk obliquely of freedom and equality. One day, she said, she would do something to bring an end to the inequities in Russian society. In the meantime, however, the empress allied herself with the nobles, gaining their support and winning more power for herself. When the peasants of Russia at last tired of waiting for Catherine to act, they took matters into their own hands. Led by Pugachev, a fiery Cossack who claimed he was Peter III come back to life, the peasants rose up against their masters and rebelled against the empress. "We are free!" they shouted. "Death to Catherine!"

The revolt, which flared up in 1773, spread throughout the provinces of Russia like a brush fire. Furious, Catherine ordered her troops to put down the peasants and to capture their leader, Pugachev. By the end of 1774, the rebellion was crushed. Pugachev was executed a year later, as were many other leaders of the unsuccessful uprising. Then, to punish the peasants, Catherine gave the landowners of Russia still more control over them, leaving the peasants more downtrodden than before. Her "children" would think twice before attempting another revolt, mused the empress.

Even after the uprising of 1773-1774, though, Catherine still toyed with the idea of one day abolishing serfdom and establishing democracy in her beloved Russia. But

A drawing of
Pugachev, leader
of the ill-fated
peasant revolt
against Catherine

after the French Revolution erupted and the rulers of France were beheaded, the empress did a complete about-face. Fearing that her restless subjects might follow the example of the French, and putting her own welfare above all else, Catherine II quickly tightened the reins on her people. What is more, she exiled those Russians who dared to parrot her youthful ideas on freedom, sending many of them to Siberia. Democracy would never come to Russia, Catherine vowed. At least not while she was still living.

Many historians have been quick to point out that Catherine II was a champion of her people *only* so long as her own power and position were not threatened. This is hard to dispute; yet, it should also be pointed out that Catherine's record of social reform is a long and impressive one—and one that shows that Catherine II did, in fact, care about her people. The empress never freed the peasants of Russia, but she saw to it that their housing and their working conditions were improved. She also saw to it that the peasants were paid for their labor by their masters, thus elevating them above the status of common slaves. So that her people might be better educated and cared for, Catherine II established free schools and hospitals throughout the provinces of Russia. Equally important, she codified the laws of Russia so that they would no longer vary from one province to another. She outlawed cruel and barbaric punishment, and ordered that all her people were to be equal in the eyes of the law, with the right to a lawyer and a fair trial. So, too, Catherine ordered that the lawyers, judges, and provincial governors of Russia be properly trained for their jobs. To this end, she herself spent many hours giving lessons on law, order, and statecraft. Catherine was a brilliant teacher, and her students learned well.

What else did Catherine II do for Russia? She (1) reformed its tax system; (2) standardized its currency; (3) took a census of its population; (4) helped free it of plagues by promoting inoculation against smallpox; (5) extended religious tolerance in it; and (6) built for it new highways, new canals, new towns, and new cities. And—still—the list of Catherine's accomplishments is not complete.

Of all Catherine's projects, her most ambitious one was probably her one-woman campaign to westernize Russia, a backward nation that was more Asiatic than European when Catherine ascended the throne. By establishing free schools for the poor, the empress went a long way in stamping out ignorance and superstition in Russia. But she wasn't satisfied; she wanted to do a great deal more for her adopted country. Eventually, Catherine decided to concentrate her efforts on St. Petersburg, then the capital of Russia.

To begin with, Empress Catherine commissioned Bartolomeo Rastrelli—one of Italy's finest architects—to expand and remodel the Winter Palace. Rastrelli worked on the mammoth building for years, finally transforming it into one of the most magnificent palaces in the world. This accomplished, Catherine recruited a team of French architects to build an art gallery next to the Winter Palace. She named it the Hermitage upon its completion, then filled it with a collection of art treasures that in-

The magnificent Hermitage, as it looks today

cluded works by Rembrandt, Raphael, and Leonardo da Vinci. The empress next had a huge library built in St. Petersburg, filling it with some 40,000 books. Then came an opera house, a university, and an academy of science and art—along with still more art galleries and still more libraries.

Gradually, St. Petersburg became one of the most celebrated cultural and intellectual centers in all Europe, rivaling even the city of Paris. Artists, scholars, architects, writers, musicians, and scientists from all over the world came to the Russian city, and all called it great. Through her hard work and determination, Catherine II had succeeded in bringing the culture and ideas of the West to Russia—or to Russia's capital, at least. Catherine's hoped-for legacy was thus assured.

At the same time that Catherine was westernizing Russia, she was also extending its borders—usually by waging war on weaker nations. An iron-fisted imperialist, Catherine II was determined to make Russia a first-class power before she died. And she succeeded. During the course of her 34-year reign, she methodically added Poland, Lithuania, the Crimea, and the Ukraine to the Russian empire. She also gained control of a long stretch of land along the Black Sea. Then, after extending Russian trade to western Europe, the empress turned her attention to Alaska, and to the fur trade there. The first Russian settlement in Alaska was founded in 1784; not long after, Russia gained complete control of the rich Alaskan fur trade. By 1796, the year of Catherine's death, Russia was indeed a "first-class power," ranking along with England and France as one of the strongest and wealthiest nations in the world.

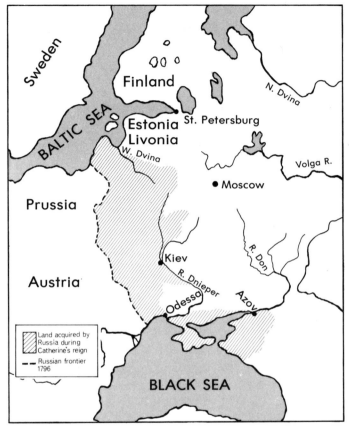

The Russian Empire in 1796, at the End of Catherine's Reign

The distinguished general and foreign adviser who helped Catherine achieve this goal was Grigori Potemkin. For a long time, he also served as the empress's most notable lover. Described as a "one-eyed, bear-like Ukrainian," Potemkin was as fond of power as Catherine was, and just as passionate. Their relationship lasted for many years, weathering many storms, but it was never sanctioned by the church. Still, it was a far more binding union than Catherine's marriage to Peter had ever been.

When Potemkin died in 1791 during a military campaign, Catherine was grief-stricken. She had loved Potemkin dearly—of that there was no doubt. Yet, one cannot help but wonder whether Potemkin would have fared any better than Catherine's other lovers had he not died a hero's death. The empress's customary way of dealing with her lovers was to banish them as soon as she found someone else she liked better. This explains why so many of her "closest" advisers were eventually stripped of all their power and position.

As Catherine II grew older, she became fat, indolent, and frustrated. Out of boredom, perhaps, the white-haired empress took up the habit of chewing snuff. Then, when she was well into her sixties, she became involved with Platon Zubov, a handsome young man nearly 40 years her junior. The affair lasted for several years, and it reduced the empress to a doting old lady.

Unfortunately, the aging Catherine received little comfort or support from her son, Grand Duke Paul. They had never been close, and Paul had grown to hate his mother through the years, largely because of her tyrannical hold on him. So, when the 67-year-old Catherine died of a stroke in 1796, her son did not mourn her passing. In fact, as Emperor Paul I, he did all he could to wipe out Catherine's memory—even to the point of leaving her tomb unadorned.

A cruel and detested ruler, Paul I was assassinated in 1801, five years after he ascended the throne. Paul was soon forgotten, but not so his illustrious mother. Despite her personal failings—and she had many of them—

Catherine II would go down in history as Catherine the Great, empress supreme. Her failings would not be forgotten, but they would be overshadowed by her long list of accomplishments. Catherine II had reigned for 34 years. In that time, she had westernized Russia, codified its laws, and made it a major world power. The autocratic system of government by which Catherine had ruled was destined to collapse, but Catherine's legacies to Russia would endure, reminding all of the greatness that was hers.

Acknowledgments

The illustrations are reproduced through the courtesy of: pp. 6, 23, Archives Photographiques, Paris; pp. 9, 33, Bibliotheque Nationales, Paris; p. 12, Walters Art Gallery; p. 15, Universitats-bibliothek, Heidelberg; pp. 16, 17, 19, 54-55, 57 (right), Mansell Collection; p. 21, reproduced by permission of the controller of Her Brittanic Majesty's Stationery Office; pp. 22, 83, British Museum; p. 24, provided and authorized by the Patrimonial Nacional; p. 27, Library of the Hispanic Society of America; p. 29, Parroco de STA Maria La Mayor, Toro; p. 34, Metropolitan Museum of Art, New York City; pp. 35, 45, reproduced by gracious permission of Her Majesty the Queen; pp. 38, 41, 47, 51, 57 (left), National Portrait Gallery, London; p. 40, Radio Times Hulton Picture Library; pp. 60, 66, 72, 75, Reunion des Musees Nationaux, Paris; p. 63 (left and right), Kunsthisches Museum; pp. 68, 69, Biblioteca Estense, Modena, Italy; p. 71, Nationalmuseum, Stockholm; p. 78, Independent Picture Service; pp. 80, 93, 95, Sovfoto; pp. 85, 90, courtesy of the Government Museum of the Union of the Soviet Socialist Republic; p. 99, Library of Congress.

Index

Place de la Revolution, 79
Plantagenet, Geoffrey (duke of Normandy), 8
Plantagenet, Henry. *See* Henry II
Poitiers Palace, 14
Potemkin, Grigori, 97-98
Princess Elisabeth. *See* Elisabeth (sister of Louis XVI)
Protestant prayerbook, 44
Puerto Rico, 36
Pugachev, 92, 93

Raleigh, Sir Walter, 56, 57
Rastrelli, Bartolomeo, 95
Raymond of Toulouse (prince of Antioch), 12
Reign of Terror, 73
religious repression: in England, 44-46; in Spain, 32-33
Richard I (king of England), 17, 18, 20-21
Richard the Lion-Hearted. *See* Richard I
Roman Catholic church: in England, 40, 44, 46, 53; in Spain, 26, 32
Romanov, Elizabeth (empress of Russia), 82, 84, 87, 88
Ropsha (country house), 91
Rosalie (servant of Marie Antoinette), 76, 77, 78
Russia, 87, 99; establishment of democracy in, 91, 92-93; expansion of, under Catherine II, 96, 97; revolution in, 89, 92; social reform in, under Catherine II, 93-94; westernization of, 94-96

Saint Petersburg, 83, 89, 90, 95-96
San Salvador, 36
serfdom, 91, 92
Seymour, Jane, 41, 42
Shakespeare, William, 56, 57
Spain, 25-26, 37; colonies of, 37; kingdoms of, 25-26, 28; unification of, 28, 29, 32, 37
Spanish Armada, 53-55; defeat of, 54-55
Spanish Inquisition, 32, 33
Spenser, Edmund, 56
Stephen (king of England), 14, 16
Stuart, James, 59
Stuart, Mary, 49, 51-52

Temple, 74-75
Third Crusade, 20
Tilbury, 53
Tower of London, 42, 46, 58
Tudor, Mary, 44-46, 47
Tuileries Palace, 74, 79
Turks, 10, 12, 20

Versailles, 65, 68
"Virginia" (British colony), 56
Voltaire (philosopher), 87, 91

Westminster Abbey, 47
William (duke of Aquitaine), 7, 8
William (son of Eleanor and Henry II), 16, 17
Windsor Palace, 16
Winter Palace, 83, 89, 90, 95
women, position of, in society, 10, 14

Zubov, Platon, 98

MARY L. DAVIS is a versatile, multi-talented woman who has worked as a teacher, a political publicist, a newspaperwoman, and a public relations account executive. Writing is her favorite pastime, and she has authored a number of books over the years. In addition to *Women Who Changed History,* Ms. Davis has written such delightful and informative children's books as *Polly and the President, Careers in Baseball,* and *Careers in a Medical Center.* She has written numerous articles for adult publications, as well.

A native of Minnesota, Ms. Davis attended the University of Minnesota as a journalism major. The author and her daughter, Laura Eileen, make their home in Minneapolis.